A Picture Book of
Thurgood Marshall

David A. Adler

illustrated by Robert Casilla

Holiday House/New York

To my dad, Sidney G. Adler, a southern historian
D. A. A.

To my loving mother, Miriam
R. C.

Text copyright © 1997 by David A. Adler
Illustrations copyright © 1997 by Robert Casilla
ALL RIGHTS RESERVED
Printed and bound in April 2015 at Tien Wah Press, Johor Bahru, Johor, Malaysia.
Library of Congress Cataloging-in-Publication Data
Adler, David A.
A picture book of Thurgood Marshall / by David A. Adler;
illustrated by Robert Casilla. —1st ed.
p. cm. — (Picture book biography)
Summary: Follows the life of the first African-American to serve
as a judge on the United States Supreme Court.
ISBN 0-8234-1308-X
1. Marshall, Thurgood, 1908–1993—Juvenile literature. 2. United
States Supreme Court—Biography—Juvenile literature. 3. Afro-
American lawyers—United States—Biography—Juvenile literature.
4. Afro-American judges—United States—Biography—Juvenile
literature. [1. Marshall, Thurgood, 1908–1993. 2. Lawyers.
3. Judges. 4. Afro-Americans—Biography.] I. Casilla, Robert,
ill. II. Title. III. Series : Adler, David A. Picture book
biography.
KF8745.M34A35   1997   96-37248   CIP   AC
347.73'26—dc21
[B]
9 10 8
ISBN-13: 978-0-8234-1308-9 (hardcover)
ISBN-13: 978-0-8234-1506-9 (paperback)

Other books in David A. Adler's *Picture Book Biography* series

Justice Thurgood Marshall was a brilliant lawyer, a leader of the Civil Rights movement, and the first African-American justice of the United States Supreme Court, the highest court in the country.

Thurgood Marshall was born on July 2, 1908, in Baltimore, Maryland, to William and Norma Marshall.

The Marshalls' first son was named William Aubrey. Their second son was named Thoroughgood after the boy's grandfather, a freed slave who served in the Union army during the Civil War. But, by the second grade, young Thoroughgood was tired of writing out such a long name. He shortened it to Thurgood.

Thurgood's father, William, worked as a dining-car waiter on the Baltimore & Ohio Railroad. Later he became a waiter at a fancy all-white country club.

William Marshall enjoyed reading about trials. When he could, he went to court and sat in the visitors gallery. Sometimes he brought Thurgood along. William Marshall was the first African American to serve on a Baltimore grand jury.

William Marshall taught his sons to debate and to prove whatever they said. Thurgood said later of his father, "He never told me to become a lawyer, but he turned me into one."

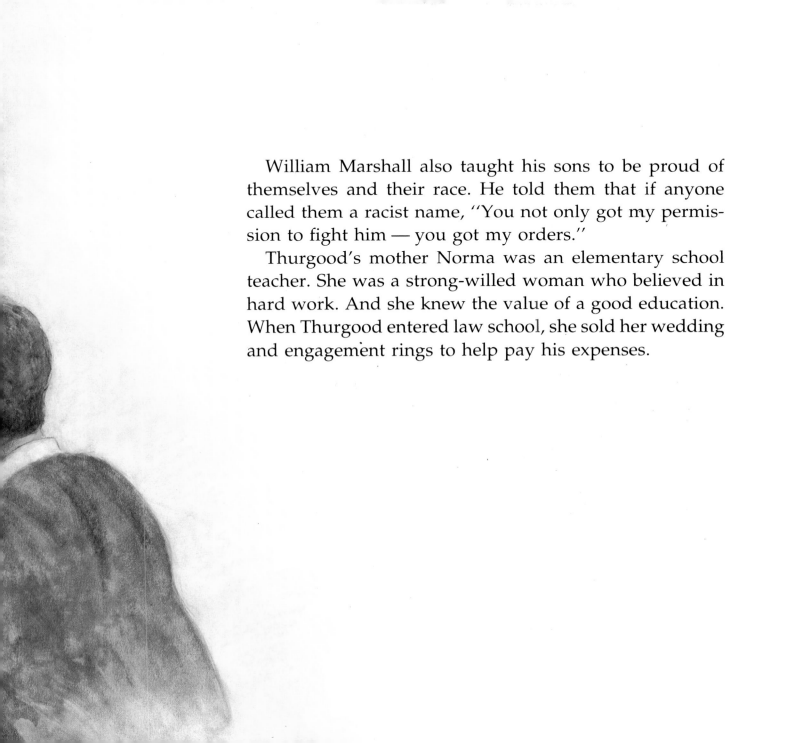

William Marshall also taught his sons to be proud of themselves and their race. He told them that if anyone called them a racist name, "You not only got my permission to fight him — you got my orders."

Thurgood's mother Norma was an elementary school teacher. She was a strong-willed woman who believed in hard work. And she knew the value of a good education. When Thurgood entered law school, she sold her wedding and engagement rings to help pay his expenses.

Young Thurgood played in the back alleys near his house. According to his relatives he was "a pretty tough guy." At school he was often in trouble. To punish him, the principal sent Thurgood to the basement with a copy of the United States Constitution. He couldn't return to class until he had memorized some of it. Thurgood Marshall said later that before he graduated, "I made my way through every paragraph."

When Thurgood Marshall was young, segregation was common. African Americans were kept apart from whites in many theaters, restaurants, hotels, parks, schools, and other public places. In 1896 the Supreme Court had declared it legal to have "separate but equal" facilities for blacks and whites.

In September 1925 Thurgood entered Lincoln University, then an all-male, all-black college in Pennsylvania. While at college, Thurgood and some African-American friends held a silent protest against segregation. They went to a movie theater and sat in the "whites only" section. Thurgood wrote later that when the movie ended, the other people didn't even look at them. "I'm not sure I like being invisible, but maybe it's better than being put to shame and not able to respect yourself."

At Lincoln, Thurgood met Vivian Burey, a student at the University of Pennsylvania. She inspired him to become a serious student.

Thurgood and Vivian planned to marry five years after they graduated, then three, and then one. But they didn't even wait that long. They married on September 4, 1929, before Thurgood began his last year of college.

Thurgood Marshall graduated Lincoln University in June 1930 with honors.

He wanted to study law at the University of Maryland. But the university was an all-white school and wouldn't admit him. He went instead to the law school at Howard University in Washington, D.C.

After his first week in school, Marshall knew that being a lawyer "was what I wanted to do for as long as I lived." He studied hard. He said later, "I heard law books were to dig in, so I dug, way deep."

Thurgood Marshall learned from all his teachers at Howard, but especially from Charles Hamilton Houston. Houston taught his students to use the law as a tool to fight segregation and discrimination.

Houston worked for the NAACP (National Association for the Advancement of Colored People). He was the first African American to win a case before the United States Supreme Court.

Thurgood Marshall graduated Howard University Law School in 1933 at the top of his class and opened a law office in Baltimore. The next year he began to work for Charles Hamilton Houston and the NAACP.

In 1935 Thurgood Marshall scored his first victory against segregation. He and Houston argued for the right of Donald Murray, an African American, to be admitted to the University of Maryland Law School. "What's at stake here," Marshall told the court, "is more than the rights of my client. It's the moral commitment stated in our country's creed."

The court ordered that Murray be admitted at once to the school that had refused Thurgood Marshall. Three years later, in 1938, Thurgood Marshall was made the chief lawyer of the NAACP.

In 1940 Thurgood Marshall argued his first case before the Supreme Court. He represented three African Americans who were accused of murder. The men had been kept in jail, away from lawyers and friends. They were asked questions for five days, almost without stop, until they confessed to the murder. Thurgood Marshall argued that the men had been forced to confess. The Supreme Court agreed.

Thurgood Marshall had won his first case before the country's highest court. He would win twenty-nine of the thirty-two cases he tried before the Supreme Court. His greatest court victory came in the case of *Brown v. Board of Education of Topeka*.

Marshall challenged the right of states to have what they claimed were "separate but equal" schools for black and white children. He told the court, "Equal means getting the same thing, at the same time, and in the same place." Separate schools could not be equal.

The Supreme Court agreed with Thurgood Marshall.

Chief Justice Earl Warren wrote that to separate a minority group from others, "solely because of their race . . . may affect their hearts and minds in a way very unlikely ever to be undone." On May 17, 1954, the court ruled to end school segregation.

The decision was a turning point in our country's history, a turning away from segregation and the terrible hardships and feelings that came with it. Thurgood Marshall said later that this ruling, more than anything else, helped to wake up African Americans to demand equality.

There was bad news, too, in 1954 for Thurgood Marshall. His wife Vivian told him she had cancer. Marshall stopped working to stay home with her. "She would have done the same for me," he said.

Vivian Burey Marshall died in February 1955.

Later that year Marshall met Cecilia Suyat, a woman who worked for the NAACP. They shared many interests and loved being together. Thurgood and Cecilia married and had two sons, Thurgood, Jr., and John.

Even after *Brown v. Board of Education of Topeka,* the end to segregation did not come quickly or easily. Thurgood Marshall continued the legal battle.

He fought in the courts against segregated housing, parks, beaches, restaurants, buses, and trains. He helped with the Montgomery, Alabama, bus boycott led by Dr. Martin Luther King, Jr.

Thurgood Marshall became known as "Mr. Civil Rights."

In 1961 Marshall was nominated by President Kennedy to be a judge on the United States Court of Appeals. It took almost a year for the Senate to approve his nomination. Four years later President Johnson appointed him United States Solicitor General, the government's top lawyer. This time the nomination was approved in just one day.

On June 13, 1967, President Johnson nominated Thurgood Marshall to be a justice on the Supreme Court. He was its first African-American judge. President Johnson said, "It is the right thing to do, the right time to do it, the right man and the right place . . . He deserves the appointment."

Thurgood Marshall was on the court for twenty-four years. He was a sure voice for human rights.

He retired in 1991 because of poor health. "I'm getting old," he said, "and coming apart."

Justice Thurgood Marshall died on January 24, 1993, at the age of eighty-four.

At a memorial service he was called, "the most significant lawyer of his time," and "a true American hero."

His casket was placed in the Supreme Court. One of the many thousands who came to say good-bye to Justice Thurgood Marshall left this note, "You will be remembered."

AUTHOR'S NOTE

Other members of Thurgood Marshall's family were strong-willed, too. His great-grandfather had been kidnapped in Central Africa and brought to America to be a slave. But he argued so often that his slaveholder set him free on the condition that he leave the county and never come back. He left slavery, but he didn't leave the county. He moved just a few miles away.

Isaiah Williams, Thurgood's maternal grandfather, organized a rally in the 1800s to protest the way Baltimore police treated African Americans.

Annie Marshall, Thurgood's paternal grandmother, stopped a Baltimore electric company from putting a light pole in front of the family's grocery store. She sat on the spot and refused to leave until they put the pole somewhere else.

IMPORTANT DATES

1908	Born in Baltimore, Maryland, on July 2.
1929	Married Vivian Burey on September 4.
1935	In *Murray v. Pearson* won the right for African Americans to attend University of Maryland Law School.
1954	Won *Brown v. Board of Education of Topeka,* ending school segregation.
1955	Wife Vivian died. Married Cecilia Suyat.
1961–1965	Judge on the U.S. Court of Appeals.
1965–1967	Served as U.S. Solicitor General.
1967–1991	Served as the first African-American justice of the United States Supreme Court.
1993	Died on January 24.